MW01283921

LIFE-CHANGING
POTATO SALADS
IN 30 MINUTES FLAT

By Grace Légere

Everyone loves potato salad and this collection of forty-seven different combinations will please just about anyone at your table. Potatoes are the perfect "blank canvas" for so many flavor profiles. These lip-smacking recipes include both traditional and super-creative options, all made fresh with your own wholesome ingredients. There are creamy ones as well as mayonnaise-free, and most are vegetarian. Some of the specialty ones even have a crunchy topping. With some simple prep techniques and a gathering of basic pantry items, all of these recipes are easy to make. The main thing to remember is that the quality of your finished product will depend completely upon the quality of your ingredients. Don't skimp on quality.

While my book's subtitle does not include the chilling time needed for the cold-style recipes, I'm sure you'll agree that when all the raw ingredients are washed and prepared ahead whenever possible, these potato salads go together in a flash. Grab a fork and get ready for some truly awesome deliciousness. You will never think of potato salad in the same way again.

~Grace Légere

TABLE OF CONTENTS

A Stocked Pantry Equals Fast Potato Salads

About potatoes

Make sure the potatoes you intend to use are firm and smooth. Ones with wrinkles, or that don't feel hard when you press them, are probably old and on their way to the afterlife. By the way, size doesn't matter but uniformity does. To insure even cooking and simultaneous doneness, make sure the potatoes you'll be boiling in the same pot are approximately the same size. To accomplish this you may have to cut any larger potatoes in half or in quarters before boiling to match the size of the smaller ones.

About mayonnaise and yogurt

For my mayonnaise-based salads, it's important you choose a brand that you and your family love. Different ones really do taste different from one another and if you choose one you are not accustomed to, it can give your potato salad a seemingly strange taste. Of course, you can always make your own mayonnaise, as you will see later. But whether you make your own or buy your favorite, it's imperative for everyone's health and safety to keep mayonnaise well-chilled. (More on that in my *Useful Tips* section)

A safer choice during the warmer months or for outdoor picnics is to choose one of my mayo-free recipes of which there are many. In a pinch, you could even switch out the mayonnaise when it is called for by replacing it with Greek style yogurt or sour cream; simply use the same measurement as indicated for the mayo. Make certain the yogurt you use is plain, not flavored.

About oils

These days there are many different types of oils available. I do indicate which I prefer in each recipe that calls for oil, but you can use whichever you have on hand. It may however subtly change the flavor of your finished potato salad. Some of the better known ones are Extra Virgin olive oil, regular olive oil, light olive oil, canola oil, peanut oil, corn oil, sunflower oil, and vegetable oil.

About vinegars

The type of vinegar you use will *greatly* impact the flavor profile so I always specify the one I prefer in any particular recipe. In general, never use white distilled vinegar — save it for cleaning your windows.

Try to learn which vinegars are sourer than others and which ones you and your loved ones enjoy most. These may include red wine vinegar, white wine vinegar, sherry vinegar, balsamic vinegar, apple cider vinegar, rice wine vinegar, and even gourmet flavored vinegars.

About citrus

When the recipe features citrus flavors, freshly squeezed juice will often act as the acid component instead of vinegar. Invest in a cook's rasp for quick, easy zesting of the fruit's flavorful outer skin; it will yield the best result. Always do your zesting *before* cutting the fruit in half to juice!

About spices and seasonings

Dried and ground spices should be replaced every year for freshness; always check any older bottled spices for critters *before* using.

About fresh herbs

Always refrigerate fresh herbs except in the case of basil, which prefers to be out on the countertop in a glass of water –like flowers in a vase. To chop fresh thyme, rosemary, or oregano, you must de-stem them first: gently pull the leaves backwards along the stem with two fingers. Many of my recipes call for fresh herbs so be certain to wash, stem, and chop them while your potatoes are boiling (or even beforehand.) Cilantro, basil, and parsley can technically be chopped up stems and all, but remove longer pieces of stem for a better and prettier potato salad.

About aromatics

Flavor-makers such as garlic, shallot, and onion should be stored in a cool, dry place and used within a week or so of purchasing. Never use one that has gone soft or is showing signs of mold. Aromatics should be firm and fragrant, and minced up within a short time of being used. Don't use nasty, pre-minced garlic jarred in oil.

About prepping chili peppers

Since I have no way of knowing your level of cooking experience I feel I should explain the handling, slicing, and chopping of hot chili peppers: your fingers will have spicy hot oil on them for some time, even after washing your hands with soap. Be careful not to touch your face, eyes, or pets until you have rewashed and waited a good amount of time. It will dissipate eventually. You could also wear latex gloves while you do the preparation thereby avoiding this problem altogether.

Also, be careful that no seeds or pieces go flying onto your kitchen floor as you are dicing and chopping chili peppers, especially if you have toddlers or dogs that like to be with you while you cook.

Choosing the Best Kind of Potato

The type of potato you use in this collection of recipes definitely matters and since it's the main ingredient you'll need to choose correctly. There are many varieties of potato in this world but for most potato salads you'll want one of the waxier varieties like Red Bliss, Yukon Gold, Fingerling, White, or New potatoes. Any young, early harvested "baby" potato is also fine. These all have thin skins which you don't have to peel if you don't want to.

I do not recommend thick-skinned Russet (Idaho) potatoes for use in my potato salads unless specifically indicated because they are simply too starchy and when cooked tend to fall apart. That's why they make such great mashed potatoes! Of course, if you only have Russets on hand and really want to use them, go ahead. But make sure not to overcook them and take care to be gentle when blending with the other ingredients.

Raw potatoes like to be kept in a cool, dark cupboard or brown paper bag. They should not be stored in a refrigerator unless you live in a very hot climate. Wash them when you first bring them home and then let them dry thoroughly before putting them into storage.

Know my Cooking Abbreviations

t.	means	*teaspoon*
T.	means	*tablespoon*
c.	means	*cup*
oz.	means	*fluid ounces*
lbs.	means	*pounds*

Useful Tips

These recipes contain exact measurements but can also be "estimated" in the mixing bowl as you become more experienced at making them. Almost all call for 2½ pounds of potatoes to approximately 1 cup of dressing, and serve six to eight persons as a salad or side dish.

Items needed:

A cooking pot with a 4- to 5-quart capacity and a lid, a small glass or metal bowl that's at least 10" in diameter, a set of proper measuring spoons, a chef's knife, a mini whisk, and a measuring cup. Two larger bowls will be needed as well, one for the icy bath that will stop the potatoes from cooking and one for the actual blending of all the ingredients.

Depending on the recipe it may also be helpful to have a cook's rasp for proper zesting of fresh citrus skin, and a small seed-catching citrus juicing strainer. A "spider" is a great tool for getting the potatoes from the boiling water to the icy bath but can be replaced by a large slotted spoon.

No need to peel.

As long as you use tender, thin-skinned potatoes there's really no reason to peel them. It's a matter of aesthetics and personal preference. If you decide you want skinless potatoes in your salad, cook them a minute longer than my instructions call for and then after the icy bath, simply slide the skins off. (Sometimes the skins come off while you are cutting them into bite-size pieces anyway. Don't fret if this happen; your potato salad will still turn out great.

Cooking the potatoes:

Run water into your pot until it reaches about two inches high from the bottom. Add one heaping tablespoon of regular iodized salt and stir. Place your same-sized spuds with the skins still on into the salted water. (Your potatoes will be either whole, halved, quartered, or a combination of the three depending on how you had to deal with their different sizes.) Cover with a proper fitting lid and place over high heat to wait for it to boil.

Once potatoes are boiling, turn down the heat to medium and cover again to simmer for fifteen minutes. Set a timer! The point of a small, sharp knife pierced into them will tell you they are tender and ready, or that they may need a few more minutes. *Smaller potatoes will be tender even before fifteen minutes so check for tenderness whenever your intuition tells you to do so.* You're the one in control and must make that very important decision. Don't overcook them.

When you and your sharp knife deem the potatoes are cooked, use a "spider" utensil to get them from the pot to the waiting bowl of ice cubes and water. This will stop them from cooking and help them to cool quickly. After three minutes in the icy water, drain them well and place on a cutting board. Slice into bite-sized pieces. (If making a warm potato salad, skip the icy bath.)

Prepare the raw ingredients beforehand.

My super-fast, thirty minute timeframe assumes your raw potatoes, fresh herbs, citrus, aromatics, and other flavorings are already washed and ready for use. (Never use dried herbs in these recipes.) Preparations like chopping or measuring can be done way beforehand, or while the potatoes simmer. Obviously, the more you can have prepped and ready, the faster it will all go together.

Whisking up your dressing ingredients:

Mayonnaise, mustards, vinaigrettes, honey, sour cream, and certain cheeses will literally bring your potatoes together while adding great flavor and texture.

A small whisk is all you need to produce a well-blended dressing which can then be added to your tender, sliced potatoes. *Whisking the dressing ingredients together helps insure even distribution of flavor on your potatoes.* Once all the other recipe ingredients are in the large bowl it will take only a few turns with a rubber spatula or wooden spoon to blend it all. Don't over mix.

To salt or not to salt?

Potatoes have a way of soaking up salt to the point where you can't even taste any. To make matters worse, there's nothing more tasteless than an unseasoned potato. I recommend using one heaping tablespoon of regular iodized salt in the simmer-water and a coarse or kosher salt for seasoning the salad *after you have sampled it.* It may not need additional salt at all! If you're observing a low salt diet, use a small amount that you can feel good about. As my mother used to say, "You can always add more salt but you can't take it away once it's in there."

Taste it!

The dressing part of the recipe provides most of the flavor profile and is flexible to the preferences and palates of those who will be enjoying it. Taste your whisked up dressing before adding it to the cut potatoes... this is the only way you'll know if it's salty enough, tart enough, spicy enough, or vinegary enough for you and your loved ones. My recipes are merely a guideline; adjust accordingly. *Note: These recipes will often yield more dressing than you'll need — add it in a bit at a time until you're satisfied with the wetness of your potato salad. Some people like it more on the drier side.*

Storing:

Potato salads can be stored in the refrigerator right in their mixing bowl, or in a decorative serving bowl with plastic wrap over the top. A clean, plastic storage container may also be used. Potato salads with ingredients like fresh herbs will keep for about a week in the refrigerator. Do not freeze!

Food safety:

Keep mayonnaise and mayonnaise-based salads properly chilled in a refrigerator. *Any brought out of refrigeration and left to become warm can bring salmonella and other life-threatening illnesses.*

How to Make Homemade Mayo

Homemade mayonnaise is easy to make and is arguably better when it's made with pure ingredients from your kitchen. It's more economical too.

1 whole egg, plus one yolk
2 t. fresh lemon juice (or apple cider vinegar)
¼ t. kosher salt, to taste
1½ t. dry mustard powder
1½ t. white granulated sugar
1 c. canola oil (or avocado oil)

Homemade mayonnaise must be prepared in a food processor or blender and then chilled immediately.

Combine the egg and extra yolk, lemon juice or vinegar, a splash of the oil, salt, sugar, and the dry mustard and blend for about two minutes. Scrape sides to insure proper mixing of ingredients. Place lid over container and restart the blades...while it's beating, slowly add the remaining oil and blend until it becomes thick and, well... mayonnaise-like. Delicious!

Yields one cup, and will keep well in the refrigerator for at least two weeks.

Americana Style

Good ol' American potato salad is infamous because it's delicious. Traditional combinations of ingredients rule in this chapter, and all the recipes are based on flavors that most Americans love.

Quick note: These recipes may yield more dressing than you'll need –add it a bit at a time until you're satisfied with the "wetness" of your potato salad. Some people like it more on the drier side, but make yours how *you* want it.

Old Fashioned Potato Salad
This resilient favorite is a perfect pairing to any family meal

2½ lbs. potatoes
3 hardboiled eggs, diced (prepared beforehand)
3 T. chopped pickles, any style you love
Half of a Vidalia onion, diced
2 stalks of fresh celery, diced

Whisk up a dressing of:
¾ c. mayonnaise
¼ c. water for thinning as desired
Freshly ground pepper, to taste
Salt only if needed

Instructions:

Place small, same-sized, thin-skinned spuds in a medium sized pot in just two inches of salted water –one heaping tablespoon of salt should be enough. If needed, cut larger potatoes in half or quarters to match the size of the smallest potatoes in your batch. Cover the pot with a proper fitting lid and place over high heat, and then wait for the water to boil.

Ready a large bowl with ice cubes and cold water to create an icy bath, and set aside.

As soon as the potatoes have started boiling, reduce the heat to medium and replace the lid. Set a timer for fifteen minutes.

While the potatoes are cooking, whisk up the dressing ingredients and then prepare all other items as indicated in the recipe (chopped, diced, minced, etc.)

Even before the timer goes off, start checking the potatoes for your desired tenderness by poking a few of them with the point of a sharp knife. If it pierces them fairly easily then they're ready. *Baby potatoes and Fingerling potatoes might be done even sooner than fifteen minutes so adjust the timing accordingly.* You're the one in control; don't overcook your potatoes.

Now firm but tender, quickly transfer them with a "spider" utensil or slotted spoon to the icy water. After three minutes, drain them thoroughly and let them dry on a cutting board. Then slice into bite-sized pieces.

Place the cut potatoes in a mixing bowl with eggs and vegetables and fold carefully with a wooden spoon or rubber spatula. Next, add the whisked dressing while continuing to gently fold everything together. Refrigerate until ready to enjoy.

My Signature Potato Salad
An indescribable flavor combination awaits you

3 lbs. potatoes
¼ c. chopped fresh parsley
3 fresh scallions, chopped

  Whisk up a dressing of:
  ¾ c. mayonnaise
  ¼ c. canola oil
  3 T. honey
  3 T. prepared yellow mustard
  1 fresh lemon, fully zested plus *half* its juice
  1 t. celery seed
  ½ t. curry powder (*this makes the dressing!*)
  ½ t. dry mustard powder
  Freshly ground pepper, to taste
  Salt only if needed

Instructions:

Place small, same-sized, thin-skinned spuds in a medium sized pot in just two inches of salted water –one heaping tablespoon of salt should be enough. If needed, cut larger potatoes in half or quarters to match the size of the smallest potatoes in your batch. Cover the pot with a proper fitting lid and place over high heat, and then wait for the water to boil.

Ready a large bowl with ice cubes and cold water to create an icy bath, and set aside.

As soon as the potatoes have started boiling, reduce the heat to medium and replace the lid. Set a timer for fifteen minutes.

While the potatoes are cooking, whisk up the dressing ingredients and then prepare all other items as indicated in the recipe (chopped, diced, minced, etc.)

Even before the timer goes off, start checking the potatoes for your desired tenderness by poking a few of them with the point of a sharp knife. If it pierces them fairly easily then they're ready. *Baby*

potatoes and Fingerling potatoes might be done even sooner than fifteen minutes so adjust the timing accordingly. You're the one in control; don't overcook your potatoes.

Now firm but tender, quickly transfer them with a "spider" utensil or slotted spoon to the icy water. After three minutes, drain them thoroughly and let them dry on a cutting board. Then slice into bite-sized pieces.

Place the cut potatoes in a mixing bowl with the other vegetables and fold carefully with a wooden spoon or rubber spatula. Next, add the whisked dressing while continuing to gently fold everything together. Refrigerate until ready to enjoy.

Classic New York Potato Salad
Creamy and mild, this is the one found in every New York delicatessen

2½ lbs. potatoes (traditionally with skins removed)
Half of a white onion, finely chopped

Whisk up a dressing of:
¾ c. mayonnaise
½ c. white wine vinegar
¼ c. water
¼ t. celery salt or celery seeds
1 T. granulated sugar
Freshly ground pepper, to taste
Salt, to taste

Instructions:

Place small, same-sized, thin-skinned spuds in a medium sized pot in just two inches of salted water –one heaping tablespoon of salt should be enough. If needed, cut larger potatoes in half or quarters to match the size of the smallest potatoes in your batch. Cover the pot with a proper fitting lid and place over high heat, and then wait for the water to boil.

Ready a large bowl with ice cubes and cold water to create an icy bath, and set aside.

As soon as the potatoes have started boiling, reduce the heat to medium and replace the lid. Set a timer for fifteen minutes.

While the potatoes are cooking, whisk up the dressing ingredients and then prepare all other items as indicated in the recipe (chopped, diced, minced, etc.)

Even before the timer goes off, start checking the potatoes for your desired tenderness by poking a few of them with the point of a sharp knife. If it pierces them fairly easily then they're ready. *Baby potatoes and Fingerling potatoes might be done even sooner than fifteen minutes so adjust the timing accordingly.* You're the one in control; don't overcook your potatoes.

Now firm but tender, quickly transfer them with a "spider" utensil or slotted spoon to the icy water. After three minutes, drain them thoroughly and let them dry on a cutting board. Then slice into bite-sized pieces.

Place the cut potatoes in a mixing bowl with the onions and fold carefully with a wooden spoon or rubber spatula. Next, add the whisked dressing while continuing to gently fold everything together. Refrigerate until ready to enjoy.

California Style Potato Salad
Veggies and mustard give this one a distinctive look

2½ lbs. potatoes
3 hardboiled eggs, diced (prepared beforehand)
½ c. chopped pickles, any style you love
Half of a red onion, diced
¼ c. chopped fresh parsley
2 fresh carrots, peeled and then grated

Whisk up a dressing of:
½ c. sour cream
¼ c. mayonnaise
2 T. white wine vinegar
2 T. prepared yellow mustard
2 T. honey
¼ t. celery seed
Freshly ground pepper, to taste
Salt, to taste

Instructions:

Place small, same-sized, thin-skinned spuds in a medium sized pot in just two inches of salted water –one heaping tablespoon of salt should be enough. If needed, cut larger potatoes in half or quarters to match the size of the smallest potatoes in your batch. Cover the pot with a proper fitting lid and place over high heat, and then wait for the water to boil.

Ready a large bowl with ice cubes and cold water to create an icy bath, and set aside.

As soon as the potatoes have started boiling, reduce the heat to medium and replace the lid. Set a timer for fifteen minutes.

While the potatoes are cooking, whisk up the dressing ingredients and then prepare all other items as indicated in the recipe (chopped, diced, minced, etc.)

Even before the timer goes off, start checking the potatoes for your desired tenderness by poking a few of them with the point of a

sharp knife. If it pierces them fairly easily then they're ready. *Baby potatoes and Fingerling potatoes might be done even sooner than fifteen minutes so adjust the timing accordingly.* You're the one in control; don't overcook your potatoes.

Now firm but tender, quickly transfer them with a "spider" utensil or slotted spoon to the icy water. After three minutes, drain them thoroughly and let them dry on a cutting board. Then slice into bite-sized pieces.

Place the cut potatoes in a mixing bowl with the eggs and vegetables and fold carefully with a wooden spoon or rubber spatula. Next, add the whisked dressing while continuing to gently fold everything together. Refrigerate until ready to enjoy.

Buffalo Blue Potato Salad
The famous flavors of upstate New York come alive

2½ lbs. potatoes
2 fresh carrots, peeled and then grated
3 stalks of fresh celery, diced
¾ c. crumbled blue cheese

Whisk up a dressing of:
¾ c. mayonnaise
1 T. white wine vinegar
¼ t. celery seeds
1 t. granulated sugar
12 shakes of good quality pepper sauce
Freshly ground pepper
Salt only if needed

Instructions:

Place small, same-sized, thin-skinned spuds in a medium sized pot in just two inches of salted water –one heaping tablespoon of salt should be enough. If needed, cut larger potatoes in half or quarters to match the size of the smallest potatoes in your batch. Cover the pot with a proper fitting lid and place over high heat, and then wait for the water to boil.

Ready a large bowl with ice cubes and cold water to create an icy bath, and set aside.

As soon as the potatoes have started boiling, reduce the heat to medium and replace the lid. Set a timer for fifteen minutes.

While the potatoes are cooking, whisk up the dressing ingredients and then prepare all other items as indicated in the recipe (chopped, diced, minced, etc.)

Even before the timer goes off, start checking the potatoes for your desired tenderness by poking a few of them with the point of a sharp knife. If it pierces them fairly easily then they're ready. *Baby potatoes and Fingerling potatoes might be done even sooner than fifteen*

minutes so adjust the timing accordingly. You're the one in control; don't overcook your potatoes.

Now firm but tender, quickly transfer them with a "spider" utensil or slotted spoon to the icy water. After three minutes, drain them thoroughly and let them dry on a cutting board. Then slice into bite-sized pieces.

Place the cut potatoes in a mixing bowl with the blue cheese and vegetables and fold carefully with a wooden spoon or rubber spatula. Next, add the whisked dressing while continuing to gently fold everything together. Refrigerate until ready to enjoy.

Totally Loaded Potato Salad
Sour cream and crispy bacon will make your tastebuds sing

Mayo free!

2½ lbs. potatoes
8 strips of bacon cooked crispy and chopped (prepared beforehand)
½ c. chopped fresh chives or scallions

Whisk up a dressing of:
1 c. sour cream
1 T. water, for thinning dressing if desired
Freshly ground pepper, to taste

1 c. grated Monterey jack cheese, *folded in last to avoid melting*

Instructions:

Place small, same-sized, thin-skinned spuds in a medium sized pot in just two inches of salted water –one heaping tablespoon of salt should be enough. If needed, cut larger potatoes in half or quarters to match the size of the smallest potatoes in your batch. Cover the pot with a proper fitting lid and place over high heat, and then wait for the water to boil.

Ready a large bowl with ice cubes and cold water to create an icy bath, and set aside.

As soon as the potatoes have started boiling, reduce the heat to medium and replace the lid. Set a timer for fifteen minutes.

While the potatoes are cooking, whisk up the dressing ingredients and then prepare all other items as indicated in the recipe (chopped, diced, minced, etc.)

Even before the timer goes off, start checking the potatoes for your desired tenderness by poking a few of them with the point of a sharp knife. If it pierces them fairly easily then they're ready. *Baby potatoes and Fingerling potatoes might be done even sooner than fifteen minutes so adjust the timing accordingly.* You're the one in control; don't overcook your potatoes.

Now firm but tender, quickly transfer them with a "spider" utensil or slotted spoon to the icy water. After three minutes, drain them thoroughly and let them dry on a cutting board. Then slice into bite-sized pieces.

Place the cut potatoes in a mixing bowl with the bacon and chives and fold carefully with a wooden spoon or rubber spatula. Next, add the whisked dressing while continuing to gently fold everything together. Once it has cooled down, fold in the jack cheese. Refrigerate until ready to enjoy.

Honey Dijon Potato Salad
Everyone's favorite combo makes this lip-smacking good

Mayo free!

2½ lbs. potatoes
3 fresh scallions, chopped
2 stalks of fresh celery, diced
1 fresh red bell pepper, diced (seeds and pith removed)

Whisk up a dressing of:
½ c. Dijon style mustard
2 T. grainy mustard
1 to 2 T. canola oil, added as needed to thin dressing
1/3 c. honey, or more to taste
Freshly ground pepper, to taste
Salt only if needed

Instructions:

Place small, same-sized, thin-skinned spuds in a medium sized pot in just two inches of salted water –one heaping tablespoon of salt should be enough. If needed, cut larger potatoes in half or quarters to match the size of the smallest potatoes in your batch. Cover the pot with a proper fitting lid and place over high heat, and then wait for the water to boil.

Ready a large bowl with ice cubes and cold water to create an icy bath, and set aside.

As soon as the potatoes have started boiling, reduce the heat to medium and replace the lid. Set a timer for fifteen minutes.

While the potatoes are cooking, whisk up the dressing ingredients and then prepare all other items as indicated in the recipe (chopped, diced, minced, etc.)

Even before the timer goes off, start checking the potatoes for your desired tenderness by poking a few of them with the point of a sharp knife. If it pierces them fairly easily then they're ready. *Baby potatoes and Fingerling potatoes might be done even sooner than fifteen*

minutes so adjust the timing accordingly. You're the one in control; don't overcook your potatoes.

Now firm but tender, quickly transfer them with a "spider" utensil or slotted spoon to the icy water. After three minutes, drain them thoroughly and let them dry on a cutting board. Then slice into bite-sized pieces.

Place the cut potatoes in a mixing bowl with the other vegetables and fold carefully with a wooden spoon or rubber spatula. Next, add the whisked dressing while continuing to gently fold everything together. Refrigerate until ready to enjoy.

Ranch-style Potato Salad
Ranch flavors blend perfectly with garden veggies

2½ lbs. potatoes
2 stalks of fresh celery, diced
2 fresh carrot, peeled and then grated
2 T. chopped fresh parsley
3 fresh scallions, chopped
½ c. chopped broccoli florets, blanched and drained (prepared beforehand)

1 c. ranch style dressing
 (or make your own ranch dressing if you have my book, *Life-Changing Salad Dressings in 3 Minutes Flat)*
Salt only if needed

Instructions:

Place small, same-sized, thin-skinned spuds in a medium sized pot in just two inches of salted water –one heaping tablespoon of salt should be enough. If needed, cut larger potatoes in half or quarters to match the size of the smallest potatoes in your batch. Cover the pot with a proper fitting lid and place over high heat, and then wait for the water to boil.

Ready a large bowl with ice cubes and cold water to create an icy bath, and set aside.

As soon as the potatoes have started boiling, reduce the heat to medium and replace the lid. Set a timer for fifteen minutes.

While the potatoes are cooking, whisk up the dressing ingredients and then prepare all other items as indicated in the recipe (chopped, diced, minced, etc.)

Even before the timer goes off, start checking the potatoes for your desired tenderness by poking a few of them with the point of a sharp knife. If it pierces them fairly easily then they're ready. *Baby potatoes and Fingerling potatoes might be done even sooner than fifteen minutes so adjust the timing accordingly.* You're the one in control; don't overcook your potatoes.

Now firm but tender, quickly transfer them with a "spider" utensil or slotted spoon to the icy water. After three minutes, drain them thoroughly and let them dry on a cutting board. Then slice into bite-sized pieces.

Place the cut potatoes in a mixing bowl with the other vegetables and fold carefully with a wooden spoon or rubber spatula. Next, add the whisked dressing while continuing to gently fold everything together. Refrigerate until ready to enjoy.

Barbecue Potato Salad
This lip-smacking combo boasts a crispy potato chip topping!

2½ lbs. potatoes
1 c. Vidalia onion, diced
1 c. loose fresh corn (or canned) sautéed until slightly charred (prepare beforehand)
2 stalks of fresh celery, diced

   Whisk up a dressing of:
   ½ c. mayonnaise
   ½ c. prepared, good quality barbeque sauce
   1 T. red wine vinegar
   Pinch cayenne pepper, to taste (hot)

½ c. Cotija or Queso Fresca cheese, shredded or crumbled and folded in last
   -Cotija cheese can be salty, so don't add additional salt until after tasting the finished potato salad. (Salting the boiling water for the raw potatoes is fine.)

Topping: 1 c. crushed potato chips, divided up to top each serving.

Instructions:

Place small, same-sized, thin-skinned spuds in a medium sized pot in just two inches of salted water –one heaping tablespoon of salt should be enough. If needed, cut larger potatoes in half or quarters to match the size of the smallest potatoes in your batch. Cover the pot with a proper fitting lid and place over high heat, and then wait for the water to boil.

Ready a large bowl with ice cubes and cold water to create an icy bath, and set aside.

As soon as the potatoes have started boiling, reduce the heat to medium and replace the lid. Set a timer for fifteen minutes.

While the potatoes are cooking, whisk up the dressing ingredients and then prepare all other items as indicated in the recipe (chopped, diced, minced, etc.)

Even before the timer goes off, start checking the potatoes for your desired tenderness by poking a few of them with the point of a sharp knife. If it pierces them fairly easily then they're ready. *Baby potatoes and Fingerling potatoes might be done even sooner than fifteen minutes so adjust the timing accordingly.* You're the one in control; don't overcook your potatoes.

Now firm but tender, quickly transfer them with a "spider" utensil or slotted spoon to the icy water. After three minutes, drain them thoroughly and let them dry on a cutting board. Then slice into bite-sized pieces.

Place the cut potatoes in a mixing bowl with the other vegetables and fold carefully with a wooden spoon or rubber spatula. Next, add the whisked dressing and cheese while continuing to gently fold everything together. Use the potato chip topping at the last minute when you are plating or presenting so that it stays crisp!

Refrigerate until ready to enjoy and then add the topping.

Fresh Dill Potato Salad
Eggs, dill, and capers make a harmonious trio

2½ lbs. potatoes
3 hardboiled eggs, diced (prepared beforehand)
1 T. capers, drained of their brine
½ c. chopped fresh dill, large stems removed

Whisk up a dressing of:
½ c. mayonnaise
½ c. sour cream
Freshly ground pepper, to taste
Salt, to taste

Instructions:

Place small, same-sized, thin-skinned spuds in a medium sized pot in just two inches of salted water –one heaping tablespoon of salt should be enough. If needed, cut larger potatoes in half or quarters to match the size of the smallest potatoes in your batch. Cover the pot with a proper fitting lid and place over high heat, and then wait for the water to boil.

Ready a large bowl with ice cubes and cold water to create an icy bath, and set aside.

As soon as the potatoes have started boiling, reduce the heat to medium and replace the lid. Set a timer for fifteen minutes.

While the potatoes are cooking, whisk up the dressing ingredients and then prepare all other items as indicated in the recipe (chopped, diced, minced, etc.)

Even before the timer goes off, start checking the potatoes for your desired tenderness by poking a few of them with the point of a sharp knife. If it pierces them fairly easily then they're ready. *Baby potatoes and Fingerling potatoes might be done even sooner than fifteen minutes so adjust the timing accordingly.* You're the one in control; don't overcook your potatoes.

Now firm but tender, quickly transfer them with a "spider" utensil or slotted spoon to the icy water. After three minutes, drain

them thoroughly and let them dry on a cutting board. Then slice into bite-sized pieces.

Place the cut potatoes in a mixing bowl with the eggs, capers, and dill and fold carefully with a wooden spoon or rubber spatula. Next, add the whisked dressing while continuing to gently fold everything together. Refrigerate until ready to enjoy.

Amish Potato Salad
A tangy dressing and crunchy vegetables make this a farm favorite

2½ lbs. potatoes
Half of a Vidalia onion, diced
3 stalks of fresh celery, diced
2 fresh carrots, peeled and then grated
3 hardboiled eggs, diced (prepared beforehand)

Whisk up a dressing of:
¾ c. mayonnaise
2 T. apple cider vinegar
1 T. sugar
1 T. prepared yellow mustard
1 t. celery seed
Freshly ground pepper, to taste
Salt, to taste

Instructions:

Place small, same-sized, thin-skinned spuds in a medium sized pot in just two inches of salted water –one heaping tablespoon of salt should be enough. If needed, cut larger potatoes in half or quarters to match the size of the smallest potatoes in your batch. Cover the pot with a proper fitting lid and place over high heat, and then wait for the water to boil.

Ready a large bowl with ice cubes and cold water to create an icy bath, and set aside.

As soon as the potatoes have started boiling, reduce the heat to medium and replace the lid. Set a timer for fifteen minutes.

While the potatoes are cooking, whisk up the dressing ingredients and then prepare all other items as indicated in the recipe (chopped, diced, minced, etc.)

Even before the timer goes off, start checking the potatoes for your desired tenderness by poking a few of them with the point of a sharp knife. If it pierces them fairly easily then they're ready. *Baby*

potatoes and Fingerling potatoes might be done even sooner than fifteen minutes so adjust the timing accordingly. You're the one in control; don't overcook your potatoes.

Now firm but tender, quickly transfer them with a "spider" utensil or slotted spoon to the icy water. After three minutes, drain them thoroughly and let them dry on a cutting board. Then slice into bite-sized pieces.

Place the cut potatoes in a mixing bowl with the eggs and vegetables and fold carefully with a wooden spoon or rubber spatula. Next, add the whisked dressing while continuing to gently fold everything together. Refrigerate until ready to enjoy.

Roasted Garlic Potato Salad
Roasted garlic brings a nutty sweetness to this one

2½ lbs. potatoes
1 c. diced roasted red peppers from a jar, drained and patted dry
2 c. fresh baby spinach, roughly chopped

Whisk up a dressing of:
½ c. mayonnaise
½ c. sour cream
Salt and freshly ground pepper, to taste
3 T. roasted garlic, prepared beforehand

> *For roasted garlic, slice ½ inch off the entire top of head with a serrated knife and then wrap it tightly in foil. Bake in a preheated 400°F (205°C) oven for 35 minutes. Cool completely before unwrapping it. The soft, oozy garlic can be squeezed right out into a measuring spoon.*

Instructions:

Place small, same-sized, thin-skinned spuds in a medium sized pot in just two inches of salted water –one heaping tablespoon of salt should be enough. If needed, cut larger potatoes in half or quarters to match the size of the smallest potatoes in your batch. Cover the pot with a proper fitting lid and place over high heat, and then wait for the water to boil.

Ready a large bowl with ice cubes and cold water to create an icy bath, and set aside.

As soon as the potatoes have started boiling, reduce the heat to medium and replace the lid. Set a timer for fifteen minutes.

While the potatoes are cooking, whisk up the dressing ingredients and then prepare all other items as indicated in the recipe (chopped, diced, minced, etc.)

Even before the timer goes off, start checking the potatoes for your desired tenderness by poking a few of them with the point of a sharp knife. If it pierces them fairly easily then they're ready. *Baby potatoes and Fingerling potatoes might be done even sooner than fifteen*

minutes so adjust the timing accordingly. You're the one in control; don't overcook your potatoes.

Now firm but tender, quickly transfer them with a "spider" utensil or slotted spoon to the icy water. After three minutes, drain them thoroughly and let them dry on a cutting board. Then slice into bite-sized pieces.

Place the cut potatoes in a mixing bowl with the diced red peppers and fold carefully with a wooden spoon or rubber spatula. Next, add the whisked dressing and chopped spinach while continuing to gently fold everything together. Refrigerate until ready to enjoy.

Southwestern Potato Salad
A sweet and smoky dressing makes potatoes irresistible

2½ lbs. potatoes
3 stalks fresh celery, diced
1 c. loose fresh corn, (or canned) sautéed until slightly charred (prepared beforehand)
½ c. diced green chilies (from a can)
Half of a red onion, diced

Whisk up a dressing of:
½ c. mayonnaise
½ c. prepared barbeque sauce
½ t. ground cumin
¼ t. ancho chili powder
1 T. olive oil
Freshly ground pepper, to taste
Salt only if needed

Instructions:

Place small, same-sized, thin-skinned spuds in a medium sized pot in just two inches of salted water –one heaping tablespoon of salt should be enough. If needed, cut larger potatoes in half or quarters to match the size of the smallest potatoes in your batch. Cover the pot with a proper fitting lid and place over high heat, and then wait for the water to boil.

Ready a large bowl with ice cubes and cold water to create an icy bath, and set aside.

As soon as the potatoes have started boiling, reduce the heat to medium and replace the lid. Set a timer for fifteen minutes.

While the potatoes are cooking, whisk up the dressing ingredients and then prepare all other items as indicated in the recipe (chopped, diced, minced, etc.)

Even before the timer goes off, start checking the potatoes for your desired tenderness by poking a few of them with the point of a sharp knife. If it pierces them fairly easily then they're ready. *Baby*

potatoes and Fingerling potatoes might be done even sooner than fifteen minutes so adjust the timing accordingly. You're the one in control; don't overcook your potatoes.

Now firm but tender, quickly transfer them with a "spider" utensil or slotted spoon to the icy water. After three minutes, drain them thoroughly and let them dry on a cutting board. Then slice into bite-sized pieces.

Place the cut potatoes in a mixing bowl with the other vegetables and fold carefully with a wooden spoon or rubber spatula. Next, add the whisked dressing while continuing to gently fold everything together. Refrigerate until ready to enjoy.

Three-Pickle Potato Salad

The balance of both sour and sweet pickles makes this one fantastic

2½ lbs. potatoes
¼ c. chopped *Bread and Butter* style pickles
¼ c. chopped Gherkin pickles
¼ c. chopped garlic-brined pickles
2 T. chopped fresh dill, large stems removed

Whisk up a dressing of:
¾ c. mayonnaise
¼ c. pickle juice
Freshly ground pepper, to taste
Salt only if needed

Instructions:

Place small, same-sized, thin-skinned spuds in a medium sized pot in just two inches of salted water –one heaping tablespoon of salt should be enough. If needed, cut larger potatoes in half or quarters to match the size of the smallest potatoes in your batch. Cover the pot with a proper fitting lid and place over high heat, and then wait for the water to boil.

Ready a large bowl with ice cubes and cold water to create an icy bath, and set aside.

As soon as the potatoes have started boiling, reduce the heat to medium and replace the lid. Set a timer for fifteen minutes.

While the potatoes are cooking, whisk up the dressing ingredients and then prepare all other items as indicated in the recipe (chopped, diced, minced, etc.)

Even before the timer goes off, start checking the potatoes for your desired tenderness by poking a few of them with the point of a sharp knife. If it pierces them fairly easily then they're ready. *Baby potatoes and Fingerling potatoes might be done even sooner than fifteen minutes so adjust the timing accordingly.* You're the one in control; don't overcook your potatoes.

Now firm but tender, quickly transfer them with a "spider" utensil or slotted spoon to the icy water. After three minutes, drain them thoroughly and let them dry on a cutting board. Then slice into bite-sized pieces.

Place the cut potatoes in a mixing bowl with the pickles and dill and fold carefully with a wooden spoon or rubber spatula. Next, add the whisked dressing while continuing to gently fold everything together. Refrigerate until ready to enjoy.

Spicy Bacon & Egg Potato Salad
Meaty umami flavors rule in this unique potato salad

Mayo free!

2½ lbs. potatoes
3 eggs beaten, seasoned, and scrambled well, then crumbled into smaller pieces
6 strips of extra thick bacon, cooked crispy and chopped (prepared beforehand)
2 fresh scallions, chopped

Whisk up a dressing of:
½ c. Hoisin sauce
¼ c. honey
1T. rice wine vinegar
2 T. soy sauce
1 T. canola oil
1 T. dry mustard powder
¼ t. dried red pepper flakes, optional (hot)
Freshly ground pepper, to taste

Serve warm, or at room temperature

Instructions:

Place small, same-sized, thin-skinned spuds in a medium sized pot in just two inches of salted water –one heaping tablespoon of salt should be enough. If needed, cut larger potatoes in half or quarters to match the size of the smallest potatoes in your batch. Cover the pot with a proper fitting lid and place over high heat, and then wait for the water to boil.

As soon as the potatoes have started boiling, reduce the heat to medium and replace the lid. Set a timer for fifteen minutes.

While the potatoes are cooking, whisk up the dressing ingredients and then prepare all other items as indicated in the recipe (chopped, diced, minced, etc.)

Even before the timer goes off, start checking the potatoes for your desired tenderness by poking a few of them with the point of a sharp knife. If it pierces them fairly easily then they're ready. *Baby potatoes and Fingerling potatoes might be done even sooner than fifteen minutes so adjust the timing accordingly.* You're the one in control; don't overcook your potatoes.

Now firm but tender, quickly transfer them with a "spider" utensil or slotted spoon to a cutting board to dry and cool down enough to touch. Then slice into bite-sized pieces.

Place the cut potatoes in a mixing bowl with the other vegetables and fold carefully with a wooden spoon or rubber spatula. Next, add the whisked dressing while continuing to gently fold everything together. Serve warm if desired.

Southern Potato Salad
Show some Southern hospitality with this flavor combo

Mayo free!

2½ lbs. potatoes
½ c. chopped cherry peppers, (from a jar) -reserve the brine
1 T. chopped fresh parsley

Whisk up a dressing of:
½ c. sour cream
½ c. softened cream cheese
1 T. brine from the cherry peppers
½ t. celery seeds
Freshly ground pepper, to taste
Salt only if needed

Topping: 1 c. grated sharp cheddar cheese, divided up to top each serving

Instructions:

Place small, same-sized, thin-skinned spuds in a medium sized pot in just two inches of salted water –one heaping tablespoon of salt should be enough. If needed, cut larger potatoes in half or quarters to match the size of the smallest potatoes in your batch. Cover the pot with a proper fitting lid and place over high heat, and then wait for the water to boil.

Ready a large bowl with ice cubes and cold water to create an icy bath, and set aside.

As soon as the potatoes have started boiling, reduce the heat to medium and replace the lid. Set a timer for fifteen minutes.

While the potatoes are cooking, whisk up the dressing ingredients and then prepare all other items as indicated in the recipe (chopped, diced, minced, etc.)

Even before the timer goes off, start checking the potatoes for your desired tenderness by poking a few of them with the point of a

sharp knife. If it pierces them fairly easily then they're ready. *Baby potatoes and Fingerling potatoes might be done even sooner than fifteen minutes so adjust the timing accordingly.* You're the one in control; don't overcook your potatoes.

Now firm but tender, quickly transfer them with a "spider" utensil or slotted spoon to the icy water. After three minutes, drain them thoroughly and let them dry on a cutting board. Then slice into bite-sized pieces.

Place the cut potatoes in a mixing bowl with the other vegetables and fold carefully with a wooden spoon or rubber spatula. Next, add the whisked dressing while continuing to gently fold everything together. Refrigerate until ready to enjoy and be sure to top with the grated cheddar on each serving.

Red Bliss Potato Salad
The delicate skin of these potatoes adds color and nutrition

Mayo-free!

2½ lbs. Red Bliss potatoes, or other red-skinned variety
3 fresh scallions, chopped
2 T. chopped fresh parsley

  Whisk up a dressing of:
  1 c. sour cream
  1 T. Dijon style mustard
  ¼ c. celery seeds
  Freshly ground pepper, to taste
  Salt, to taste

Instructions:

Place small, same-sized, thin-skinned spuds in a medium sized pot in just two inches of salted water –one heaping tablespoon of salt should be enough. If needed, cut larger potatoes in half or quarters to match the size of the smallest potatoes in your batch. Cover the pot with a proper fitting lid and place over high heat, and then wait for the water to boil.

Ready a large bowl with ice cubes and cold water to create an icy bath, and set aside.

As soon as the potatoes have started boiling, reduce the heat to medium and replace the lid. Set a timer for fifteen minutes.

While the potatoes are cooking, whisk up the dressing ingredients and then prepare all other items as indicated in the recipe (chopped, diced, minced, etc.)

Even before the timer goes off, start checking the potatoes for your desired tenderness by poking a few of them with the point of a sharp knife. If it pierces them fairly easily then they're ready. *Baby potatoes and Fingerling potatoes might be done even sooner than fifteen minutes so adjust the timing accordingly.* You're the one in control; don't overcook your potatoes.

Now firm but tender, quickly transfer them with a "spider" utensil or slotted spoon to the icy water. After three minutes, drain them thoroughly and let them dry on a cutting board. Then slice into bite-sized pieces.

Place the cut potatoes in a mixing bowl with the other vegetables and fold carefully with a wooden spoon or rubber spatula. Next, add the whisked dressing while continuing to gently fold everything together. Refrigerate until ready to enjoy.

Yukon Gold Potato Salad
Fingerling potatoes can also be used in this easy preparation

Mayo free!

2½ lbs. Yukon Gold potatoes
2 stalks fresh celery, diced small
1 T. capers, drained of their brine

Whisk up a dressing of:
  ¾ c. olive oil
  ¼ c. Champagne vinegar
  1 T. honey
  2 T. chopped fresh thyme
  Freshly ground pepper, to taste
  Salt, to taste

Instructions:

Place small, same-sized, thin-skinned spuds in a medium sized pot in just two inches of salted water –one heaping tablespoon of salt should be enough. If needed, cut larger potatoes in half or quarters to match the size of the smallest potatoes in your batch. Cover the pot with a proper fitting lid and place over high heat, and then wait for the water to boil.

Ready a large bowl with ice cubes and cold water to create an icy bath, and set aside.

As soon as the potatoes have started boiling, reduce the heat to medium and replace the lid. Set a timer for fifteen minutes.

While the potatoes are cooking, whisk up the dressing ingredients and then prepare all other items as indicated in the recipe (chopped, diced, minced, etc.)

Even before the timer goes off, start checking the potatoes for your desired tenderness by poking a few of them with the point of a sharp knife. If it pierces them fairly easily then they're ready. *Baby potatoes and Fingerling potatoes might be done even sooner than fifteen*

minutes so adjust the timing accordingly. You're the one in control; don't overcook your potatoes.

Now firm but tender, quickly transfer them with a "spider" utensil or slotted spoon to the icy water. After three minutes, drain them thoroughly and let them dry on a cutting board. Then slice into bite-sized pieces.

Place the cut potatoes in a mixing bowl with the celery and capers and fold carefully with a wooden spoon or rubber spatula. Next, add the whisked dressing while continuing to gently fold everything together. Refrigerate until ready to enjoy.

European
recipes
next!

Mediterranean Style

The cherished flavors of the Mediterranean lend themselves well to potato salads. Many of these are mayo-free and you won't miss it a bit. Find a flavor profile you love and start cooking!

[Be careful with your salt in all of these Mediterranean style recipes... many of the ingredients will bring saltiness to the recipe without you adding more to the finished dish, especially parmesan and Romano cheeses, gorgonzola, olives, and salami. Taste it, and then decide.]

Quick note: These recipes may yield more dressing than you'll need –add it a bit at a time until you're satisfied with the "wetness" of your potato salad. Some people like it more on the drier side, but make yours how *you* want it.

Lemon Mediterranean Potato Salad
With the bright taste of fresh herbs and olives

Mayo free!

2½ lbs. potatoes
12 cherry tomatoes, halved
12 marinated, pitted green olives, drained of their brine and sliced
1 T. capers, drained of their brine
1 T. chopped fresh parsley

  Whisk up a dressing of:
  ½ c. extra virgin olive oil
  2 T. red wine vinegar
  1 lemon, fully zested plus all its juice
  3 cloves fresh garlic, finely chopped
  1 t. Dijon style mustard
  2 t. sugar
  6 to 8 fresh basil leaves, sliced chiffonade style
  1 T. chopped fresh oregano, stems removed
  Freshly ground pepper, to taste
  Add salt to taste only if needed

Instructions:

Place small, same-sized, thin-skinned spuds in a medium sized pot in just two inches of salted water –one heaping tablespoon of salt should be enough. If needed, cut larger potatoes in half or quarters to match the size of the smallest potatoes in your batch. Cover the pot with a proper fitting lid and place over high heat, and then wait for the water to boil.

Ready a large bowl with ice cubes and cold water to create an icy bath, and set aside.

As soon as the potatoes have started boiling, reduce the heat to medium and replace the lid. Set a timer for fifteen minutes.

While the potatoes are cooking, whisk up the dressing ingredients and then prepare all other items as indicated in the recipe (chopped, diced, minced, etc.)

Even before the timer goes off, start checking the potatoes for your desired tenderness by poking a few of them with the point of a sharp knife. If it pierces them fairly easily then they're ready. *Baby potatoes and Fingerling potatoes might be done even sooner than fifteen minutes so adjust the timing accordingly.* You're the one in control; don't overcook your potatoes.

Now firm but tender, quickly transfer them with a "spider" utensil or slotted spoon to the icy water. After three minutes, drain them thoroughly and let them dry on a cutting board. Then slice into bite-sized pieces.

Place the cut potatoes in a mixing bowl with the other vegetables and fold carefully with a wooden spoon or rubber spatula. Next, add the whisked dressing while continuing to gently fold everything together. Refrigerate until ready to enjoy.

Parmesan Artichoke Potato Salad
A natural combination you won't soon forget

Mayo free!

2½ lbs. potatoes
1 c. jarred or canned artichoke hearts, drained and cut into chunks
¼ c. finely grated parmesan cheese

Whisk up a dressing of:
1 c. Greek style yogurt
1 T. white wine vinegar
1 lemon, fully zested plus all its juice
3 cloves fresh garlic, minced
1 t. sugar
1 T. chopped fresh parsley
Freshly ground pepper, to taste
Add salt to taste only if needed

Instructions:

Place small, same-sized, thin-skinned spuds in a medium sized pot in just two inches of salted water –one heaping tablespoon of salt should be enough. If needed, cut larger potatoes in half or quarters to match the size of the smallest potatoes in your batch. Cover the pot with a proper fitting lid and place over high heat, and then wait for the water to boil.

Ready a large bowl with ice cubes and cold water to create an icy bath, and set aside.

As soon as the potatoes have started boiling, reduce the heat to medium and replace the lid. Set a timer for fifteen minutes.

While the potatoes are cooking, whisk up the dressing ingredients and then prepare all other items as indicated in the recipe (chopped, diced, minced, etc.)

Even before the timer goes off, start checking the potatoes for your desired tenderness by poking a few of them with the point of a sharp knife. If it pierces them fairly easily then they're ready. *Baby*

potatoes and Fingerling potatoes might be done even sooner than fifteen minutes so adjust the timing accordingly. You're the one in control; don't overcook your potatoes.

Now firm but tender, quickly transfer them with a "spider" utensil or slotted spoon to the icy water. After three minutes, drain them thoroughly and let them dry on a cutting board. Then slice into bite-sized pieces.

Place the cut potatoes in a mixing bowl with the artichokes and parmesan cheese and fold carefully with a wooden spoon or rubber spatula. Next, add the whisked dressing while continuing to gently fold everything together. Refrigerate until ready to enjoy.

Italian Pesto Potato Salad
The classic sauce makes a great potato salad

Mayo free!

2½ lbs. potatoes
12 fresh cherry tomatoes, halved
1 shallot, chopped
1 c. chopped fresh baby arugula

Whisk up a dressing of:
¾ c. basil pesto (good quality or homemade)
¼ c. light olive oil to thin the pesto, if desired
Freshly ground pepper, to taste
Add salt to taste only if needed

Topping: 2 T. toasted pine nuts divided up to top each serving

Instructions:

Place small, same-sized, thin-skinned spuds in a medium sized pot in just two inches of salted water –one heaping tablespoon of salt should be enough. If needed, cut larger potatoes in half or quarters to match the size of the smallest potatoes in your batch. Cover the pot with a proper fitting lid and place over high heat, and then wait for the water to boil.

Ready a large bowl with ice cubes and cold water to create an icy bath, and set aside.

As soon as the potatoes have started boiling, reduce the heat to medium and replace the lid. Set a timer for fifteen minutes.

While the potatoes are cooking, whisk up the dressing ingredients and then prepare all other items as indicated in the recipe (chopped, diced, minced, etc.)

Even before the timer goes off, start checking the potatoes for your desired tenderness by poking a few of them with the point of a sharp knife. If it pierces them fairly easily then they're ready. *Baby potatoes and Fingerling potatoes might be done even sooner than fifteen*

minutes so adjust the timing accordingly. You're the one in control; don't overcook your potatoes.

Now firm but tender, quickly transfer them with a "spider" utensil or slotted spoon to the icy water. After three minutes, drain them thoroughly and let them dry on a cutting board. Then slice into bite-sized pieces.

Place the cut potatoes in a mixing bowl with the other vegetables and fold carefully with a wooden spoon or rubber spatula. Next, add the whisked dressing while continuing to gently fold everything together. Refrigerate until ready to enjoy and then top with pine nuts on each serving.

Greek Potato Salad
Olives and herbs blend with feta cheese in this special dish

Mayo free!

2½ lbs. potatoes
½ c. chopped fresh oregano, stems removed
12 marinated, pitted Kalamata olives, sliced
½ c. chopped fresh parsley

Whisk up a dressing of:
¾ c. extra virgin olive oil
¼ c. red wine vinegar
3 fresh garlic cloves, minced
1 t. sugar
Freshly ground pepper, to taste

Topping: ¾ c. crumbled Feta cheese (imported preferred) added last

Instructions:

Place small, same-sized, thin-skinned spuds in a medium sized pot in just two inches of salted water –one heaping tablespoon of salt should be enough. If needed, cut larger potatoes in half or quarters to match the size of the smallest potatoes in your batch. Cover the pot with a proper fitting lid and place over high heat, and then wait for the water to boil.

Ready a large bowl with ice cubes and cold water to create an icy bath, and set aside.

As soon as the potatoes have started boiling, reduce the heat to medium and replace the lid. Set a timer for fifteen minutes.

While the potatoes are cooking, whisk up the dressing ingredients and then prepare all other items as indicated in the recipe (chopped, diced, minced, etc.)

Even before the timer goes off, start checking the potatoes for your desired tenderness by poking a few of them with the point of a

sharp knife. If it pierces them fairly easily then they're ready. *Baby potatoes and Fingerling potatoes might be done even sooner than fifteen minutes so adjust the timing accordingly.* You're the one in control; don't overcook your potatoes.

Now firm but tender, quickly transfer them with a "spider" utensil or slotted spoon to the icy water. After three minutes, drain them thoroughly and let them dry on a cutting board. Then slice into bite-sized pieces.

Place the cut potatoes in a mixing bowl with the herbs and olives and fold carefully with a wooden spoon or rubber spatula. Next, add the whisked dressing while continuing to gently fold everything together. Refrigerate until ready to enjoy and then top with crumbled Feta on each serving.

Tzatziki Potato Salad
The famous Greek sauce is luscious on potatoes

Mayo free!

2½ lbs. potatoes
Half of an *English* cucumber (for fewer seeds), peeled and diced
2 T. diced roasted red peppers (from a jar)

Whisk up a dressing of:
1 c. plain Greek style yogurt
2 T. chopped fresh dill
4 cloves fresh garlic, minced
1 T. extra virgin olive oil
1 T. honey, if desired
Freshly ground pepper, to taste
Add salt to taste only if needed

Instructions:

Place small, same-sized, thin-skinned spuds in a medium sized pot in just two inches of salted water –one heaping tablespoon of salt should be enough. If needed, cut larger potatoes in half or quarters to match the size of the smallest potatoes in your batch. Cover the pot with a proper fitting lid and place over high heat, and then wait for the water to boil.

Ready a large bowl with ice cubes and cold water to create an icy bath, and set aside.

As soon as the potatoes have started boiling, reduce the heat to medium and replace the lid. Set a timer for fifteen minutes.

While the potatoes are cooking, whisk up the dressing ingredients and then prepare all other items as indicated in the recipe (chopped, diced, minced, etc.)

Even before the timer goes off, start checking the potatoes for your desired tenderness by poking a few of them with the point of a sharp knife. If it pierces them fairly easily then they're ready. *Baby potatoes and Fingerling potatoes might be done even sooner than fifteen*

minutes so adjust the timing accordingly. You're the one in control; don't overcook your potatoes.

Now firm but tender, quickly transfer them with a "spider" utensil or slotted spoon to the icy water. After three minutes, drain them thoroughly and let them dry on a cutting board. Then slice into bite-sized pieces.

Place the cut potatoes in a mixing bowl with the other vegetables and fold carefully with a wooden spoon or rubber spatula. Next, add the whisked dressing while continuing to gently fold everything together. Refrigerate until ready to enjoy.

Creamy Romano Potato Salad
Intense Pecorino Romano adds a mouth-watering depth of flavor

2½ lbs. potatoes
1 c. chopped fresh Vidalia onion
3 T. chopped fresh parsley
1 c. chopped fresh baby arugula

Whisk up a dressing of:
1 c. mayonnaise
¾ c. finely grated, imported Pecorino Romano cheese
¼ c. water, if needed to thin dressing
Freshly ground pepper to taste (no salt should be needed!)

Instructions:

Place small, same-sized, thin-skinned spuds in a medium sized pot in just two inches of salted water –one heaping tablespoon of salt should be enough. If needed, cut larger potatoes in half or quarters to match the size of the smallest potatoes in your batch. Cover the pot with a proper fitting lid and place over high heat, and then wait for the water to boil.

Ready a large bowl with ice cubes and cold water to create an icy bath, and set aside.

As soon as the potatoes have started boiling, reduce the heat to medium and replace the lid. Set a timer for fifteen minutes.

While the potatoes are cooking, whisk up the dressing ingredients and then prepare all other items as indicated in the recipe (chopped, diced, minced, etc.)

Even before the timer goes off, start checking the potatoes for your desired tenderness by poking a few of them with the point of a sharp knife. If it pierces them fairly easily then they're ready. *Baby potatoes and Fingerling potatoes might be done even sooner than fifteen minutes so adjust the timing accordingly.* You're the one in control; don't overcook your potatoes.

Now firm but tender, quickly transfer them with a "spider" utensil or slotted spoon to the icy water. After three minutes, drain them thoroughly and let them dry on a cutting board. Then slice into bite-sized pieces.

Place the cut potatoes in a mixing bowl with the arugula, onion, and parsley and fold carefully with a wooden spoon or rubber spatula. Next, add the whisked dressing while continuing to gently fold everything together. Refrigerate until ready to enjoy.

Crispy Prosciutto Potato Salad with Sundried Tomatoes
Salty, earthy flavors transform ordinary potatoes

Mayo free!

2½ lbs. potatoes
¼ lb. prosciutto ham, sautéed until crispy and drained (prepared beforehand)
10 sundried tomatoes (jarred in oil) drained and roughly chopped
¾ c. finely grated Pecorino Romano cheese (imported preferred)

Whisk up a dressing of:
¾ c. olive oil
4 to 5 T. white wine vinegar
1 T. honey
Freshly ground pepper, to taste (no salt should be needed!)

Topping: ½ c. fresh basil, sliced chiffonade style, divided up to top each serving

Serve warm or at room temperature

Instructions:

Place small, same-sized, thin-skinned spuds in a medium sized pot in just two inches of salted water –one heaping tablespoon of salt should be enough. If needed, cut larger potatoes in half or quarters to match the size of the smallest potatoes in your batch. Cover the pot with a proper fitting lid and place over high heat, and then wait for the water to boil.

As soon as the potatoes have started boiling, reduce the heat to medium and replace the lid. Set a timer for fifteen minutes.

While the potatoes are cooking, whisk up the dressing ingredients and then prepare all other items as indicated in the recipe (chopped, diced, minced, etc.)

Even before the timer goes off, start checking the potatoes for your desired tenderness by poking a few of them with the point of a sharp knife. If it pierces them fairly easily then they're ready. *Baby*

potatoes and Fingerling potatoes might be done even sooner than fifteen minutes so adjust the timing accordingly. You're the one in control; don't overcook your potatoes.

Now firm but tender, quickly transfer them with a "spider" utensil or slotted spoon to a cutting board to dry and cool down enough to touch. Then slice into bite-sized pieces.

Place the cut potatoes in a mixing bowl with the other vegetables and fold carefully with a wooden spoon or rubber spatula. Next, add the whisked dressing while continuing to gently fold everything together. Serve warm if desired and top each serving with the basil.

Garlic Aioli Potato Salad
If you love garlic, this is the one for you

2½ lbs. potatoes
3 T. chopped fresh parsley
10 jarred, sundried tomatoes (packed in oil) drained and roughly chopped
1 T. capers, drained of their brine
1 c. chopped fresh baby arugula

Whisk up a dressing of:
¾ c. mayonnaise
2 T. white wine vinegar
1 t. sugar
6 cloves fresh garlic, finely minced
Freshly ground pepper, to taste
Add salt to taste only if needed

Instructions:

Place small, same-sized, thin-skinned spuds in a medium sized pot in just two inches of salted water –one heaping tablespoon of salt should be enough. If needed, cut larger potatoes in half or quarters to match the size of the smallest potatoes in your batch. Cover the pot with a proper fitting lid and place over high heat, and then wait for the water to boil.

Ready a large bowl with ice cubes and cold water to create an icy bath, and set aside.

As soon as the potatoes have started boiling, reduce the heat to medium and replace the lid. Set a timer for fifteen minutes.

While the potatoes are cooking, whisk up the dressing ingredients and then prepare all other items as indicated in the recipe (chopped, diced, minced, etc.)

Even before the timer goes off, start checking the potatoes for your desired tenderness by poking a few of them with the point of a sharp knife. If it pierces them fairly easily then they're ready. *Baby potatoes and Fingerling potatoes might be done even sooner than fifteen*

minutes so adjust the timing accordingly. You're the one in control; don't overcook your potatoes.

Now firm but tender, quickly transfer them with a "spider" utensil or slotted spoon to the icy water. After three minutes, drain them thoroughly and let them dry on a cutting board. Then slice into bite-sized pieces.

Place the cut potatoes in a mixing bowl with the other vegetables and fold carefully with a wooden spoon or rubber spatula. Next, add the whisked dressing while continuing to gently fold everything together. Refrigerate until ready to enjoy.

Red Wine Vinaigrette Potato Salad
Super delicious and nutritious, with the crunch of fennel

Mayo free!

2½ lbs. potatoes
1 c. thinly sliced fresh, white fennel bulb (core removed!)
2 T. chopped fresh fennel fronds (the green fuzzy part)
1 c. chopped fresh baby spinach

  Whisk up a dressing of:
  ½ c. extra virgin olive oil
  3 to 4 T. red wine vinegar
  1 T. Dijon style mustard
  2 to 3 cloves fresh garlic, finely chopped
  2 t. honey
  Freshly ground pepper, to taste
  Add salt to taste only if needed

Instructions:

Place small, same-sized, thin-skinned spuds in a medium sized pot in just two inches of salted water –one heaping tablespoon of salt should be enough. If needed, cut larger potatoes in half or quarters to match the size of the smallest potatoes in your batch. Cover the pot with a proper fitting lid and place over high heat, and then wait for the water to boil.

Ready a large bowl with ice cubes and cold water to create an icy bath, and set aside.

As soon as the potatoes have started boiling, reduce the heat to medium and replace the lid. Set a timer for fifteen minutes.

While the potatoes are cooking, whisk up the dressing ingredients and then prepare all other items as indicated in the recipe (chopped, diced, minced, etc.)

Even before the timer goes off, start checking the potatoes for your desired tenderness by poking a few of them with the point of a

sharp knife. If it pierces them fairly easily then they're ready. *Baby potatoes and Fingerling potatoes might be done even sooner than fifteen minutes so adjust the timing accordingly.* You're the one in control; don't overcook your potatoes.

Now firm but tender, quickly transfer them with a "spider" utensil or slotted spoon to the icy water. After three minutes, drain them thoroughly and let them dry on a cutting board. Then slice into bite-sized pieces.

Place the cut potatoes in a mixing bowl with the other vegetables and fold carefully with a wooden spoon or rubber spatula. Next, add the whisked dressing while continuing to gently fold everything together. Refrigerate until ready to enjoy.

Primavera Potato Salad
Fresh oregano enhances vegetables in this lovely mélange

Mayo free!

2½ lbs. potatoes
1 c. chopped broccoli florets, blanched and drained (prepared beforehand)
10 cherry tomatoes, halved
1 c. loose cooked corn, drained
10 marinated, pitted black or green olives, sliced
1 c. chopped fresh baby spinach

> *Whisk up a dressing of:*
> ½ c. extra virgin olive oil
> 3 to 4 T. sherry vinegar
> 1 T. Dijon style mustard
> 2 to 3 cloves fresh garlic, finely chopped
> 1 T. chopped fresh oregano, stems removed
> 1 T. honey
> Freshly ground pepper, to taste
> Add salt to taste only if needed

Instructions:

Place small, same-sized, thin-skinned spuds in a medium sized pot in just two inches of salted water –one heaping tablespoon of salt should be enough. If needed, cut larger potatoes in half or quarters to match the size of the smallest potatoes in your batch. Cover the pot with a proper fitting lid and place over high heat, and then wait for the water to boil.

Ready a large bowl with ice cubes and cold water to create an icy bath, and set aside.

As soon as the potatoes have started boiling, reduce the heat to medium and replace the lid. Set a timer for fifteen minutes.

While the potatoes are cooking, whisk up the dressing ingredients and then prepare all other items as indicated in the recipe (chopped, diced, minced, etc.)

Even before the timer goes off, start checking the potatoes for your desired tenderness by poking a few of them with the point of a sharp knife. If it pierces them fairly easily then they're ready. *Baby potatoes and Fingerling potatoes might be done even sooner than fifteen minutes so adjust the timing accordingly.* You're the one in control; don't overcook your potatoes.

Now firm but tender, quickly transfer them with a "spider" utensil or slotted spoon to the icy water. After three minutes, drain them thoroughly and let them dry on a cutting board. Then slice into bite-sized pieces.

Place the cut potatoes in a mixing bowl with the other vegetables and fold carefully with a wooden spoon or rubber spatula. Next, add the whisked dressing while continuing to gently fold everything together. Refrigerate until ready to enjoy.

Gorgonzola Potato Salad
This piquant salad has big flavor and a surprise topping

2½ lbs. potatoes
2 T. capers, drained of their brine
1 c. chopped fresh baby arugula

   Whisk up a dressing of:
   ¾ c. mayonnaise
   ¼ water for thinning dressing, if desired
   1 c. softened, crumbled Gorgonzola cheese
   Freshly ground pepper, to taste

Topping: 4 T. crushed, smokehouse almonds, divided up to top each serving

Instructions:

Place small, same-sized, thin-skinned spuds in a medium sized pot in just two inches of salted water –one heaping tablespoon of salt should be enough. If needed, cut larger potatoes in half or quarters to match the size of the smallest potatoes in your batch. Cover the pot with a proper fitting lid and place over high heat, and then wait for the water to boil.

Ready a large bowl with ice cubes and cold water to create an icy bath, and set aside.

As soon as the potatoes have started boiling, reduce the heat to medium and replace the lid. Set a timer for fifteen minutes.

While the potatoes are cooking, whisk up the dressing ingredients and then prepare all other items as indicated in the recipe (chopped, diced, minced, etc.)

Even before the timer goes off, start checking the potatoes for your desired tenderness by poking a few of them with the point of a sharp knife. If it pierces them fairly easily then they're ready. *Baby potatoes and Fingerling potatoes might be done even sooner than fifteen minutes so adjust the timing accordingly.* You're the one in control; don't overcook your potatoes.

Now firm but tender, quickly transfer them with a "spider" utensil or slotted spoon to the icy water. After three minutes, drain them thoroughly and let them dry on a cutting board. Then slice into bite-sized pieces.

Place the cut potatoes in a mixing bowl with the capers and arugula and fold carefully with a wooden spoon or rubber spatula. Next, add the whisked dressing while continuing to gently fold everything together. Refrigerate until ready to enjoy and then top with the almonds.

Balsamic Purple Potato Salad
Baby purple potatoes lend a deep color to this one

Mayo free!

2½ lbs. purple new potatoes
3 fresh scallions, chopped
10 seedless purple grapes, halved

 Whisk up a dressing of:
 ½ c. extra virgin olive oil
 3 to 4 T. aged balsamic vinegar
 2 cloves fresh garlic, minced
 1 T. Dijon style mustard
 1 t. honey
 Salt and freshly ground pepper, to taste

Instructions:

Place small, same-sized, thin-skinned spuds in a medium sized pot in just two inches of salted water –one heaping tablespoon of salt should be enough. If needed, cut larger potatoes in half or quarters to match the size of the smallest potatoes in your batch. Cover the pot with a proper fitting lid and place over high heat, and then wait for the water to boil.

Ready a large bowl with ice cubes and cold water to create an icy bath, and set aside.

As soon as the potatoes have started boiling, reduce the heat to medium and replace the lid. Set a timer for fifteen minutes.

While the potatoes are cooking, whisk up the dressing ingredients and then prepare all other items as indicated in the recipe (chopped, diced, minced, etc.)

Even before the timer goes off, start checking the potatoes for your desired tenderness by poking a few of them with the point of a sharp knife. If it pierces them fairly easily then they're ready. *Baby potatoes and Fingerling potatoes might be done even sooner than fifteen*

minutes so adjust the timing accordingly. You're the one in control; don't overcook your potatoes.

Now firm but tender, quickly transfer them with a "spider" utensil or slotted spoon to the icy water. After three minutes, drain them thoroughly and let them dry on a cutting board. Then slice into bite-sized pieces.

Place the cut potatoes in a mixing bowl with the grapes and scallions and fold carefully with a wooden spoon or rubber spatula. Next, add the whisked dressing while continuing to gently fold everything together. Refrigerate until ready to enjoy.

Pizzaiola Potato Salad
Favorite pizza toppings bring Italy to your table

Mayo free!

2½ lbs. potatoes
12 "grape" tomatoes, halved
1 c. Italian salami, diced
1 fresh green bell pepper, diced, with pith removed
½ c. chopped fresh Vidalia onion

Whisk up a dressing of:
¾ c. extra virgin olive oil
3 to 4 T. red wine vinegar
3 cloves fresh garlic, minced
1 T. honey
1 T. chopped fresh oregano, stems removed
¼ t. dried red pepper flakes, optional (hot)
Freshly ground pepper, to taste
Add salt to taste only if needed

Topping: 1 c. shredded mozzarella cheese, divided up to top each serving

Instructions:

Place small, same-sized, thin-skinned spuds in a medium sized pot in just two inches of salted water –one heaping tablespoon of salt should be enough. If needed, cut larger potatoes in half or quarters to match the size of the smallest potatoes in your batch. Cover the pot with a proper fitting lid and place over high heat, and then wait for the water to boil.

Ready a large bowl with ice cubes and cold water to create an icy bath, and set aside.

As soon as the potatoes have started boiling, reduce the heat to medium and replace the lid. Set a timer for fifteen minutes.

While the potatoes are cooking, whisk up the dressing ingredients and then prepare all other items as indicated in the recipe (chopped, diced, minced, etc.)

Even before the timer goes off, start checking the potatoes for your desired tenderness by poking a few of them with the point of a sharp knife. If it pierces them fairly easily then they're ready. *Baby potatoes and Fingerling potatoes might be done even sooner than fifteen minutes so adjust the timing accordingly.* You're the one in control; don't overcook your potatoes.

Now firm but tender, quickly transfer them with a "spider" utensil or slotted spoon to the icy water. After three minutes, drain them thoroughly and let them dry on a cutting board. Then slice into bite-sized pieces.

Place the cut potatoes in a mixing bowl with the vegetables and salami and fold carefully with a wooden spoon or rubber spatula. Next, add the whisked dressing while continuing to gently fold everything together. Refrigerate until ready to enjoy and then top with the shredded cheese.

More
European
flavors
coming up!

French Style

The French have been culinary masters for centuries and the particular flavor combinations they love best make for some super delicious potato salads. Check these out and see if your mouth doesn't water!

Quick note: These recipes may yield more dressing than you'll need –add it a bit at a time until you're satisfied with the "wetness" of your potato salad. Some people like it more on the drier side, but make yours how *you* want it.

French Potato Salad with Chèvre
Fresh goat cheese lends a piquant touch to this creamy blend

2½ lbs. potatoes
1 small fresh shallot, finely chopped
12 fresh, pitted cherries, sliced, rinsed, and drained

  Whisk up a dressing of:
  ½ c. mayonnaise
  ½ c. sour cream
  ¾ c. crumbled goat cheese, softened
  1 T. white wine vinegar
  2 cloves fresh garlic, finely chopped
  2 T. honey
  Freshly ground pepper, to taste
  Add salt to taste only if needed

Instructions:

   Place small, same-sized, thin-skinned spuds in a medium sized pot in just two inches of salted water –one heaping tablespoon of salt should be enough. If needed, cut larger potatoes in half or quarters to match the size of the smallest potatoes in your batch. Cover the pot with a proper fitting lid and place over high heat, and then wait for the water to boil.

   Ready a large bowl with ice cubes and cold water to create an icy bath, and set aside.

As soon as the potatoes have started boiling, reduce the heat to medium and replace the lid. Set a timer for fifteen minutes.

While the potatoes are cooking, whisk up the dressing ingredients and then prepare all other items as indicated in the recipe (chopped, diced, minced, etc.)

Even before the timer goes off, start checking the potatoes for your desired tenderness by poking a few of them with the point of a sharp knife. If it pierces them fairly easily then they're ready. *Baby potatoes and Fingerling potatoes might be done even sooner than fifteen minutes so adjust the timing accordingly.* You're the one in control; don't overcook your potatoes.

Now firm but tender, quickly transfer them with a "spider" utensil or slotted spoon to the icy water. After three minutes, drain them thoroughly and let them dry on a cutting board. Then slice into bite-sized pieces.

Place the cut potatoes in a mixing bowl with the shallots and cherries and fold carefully with a wooden spoon or rubber spatula. Next, add the whisked dressing while continuing to gently fold everything together. Refrigerate until ready to enjoy.

Champagne Dijon Potato Salad
A truly elegant and satisfying side dish

Mayo free!

2½ lbs. Yukon Gold potatoes
2 T. chopped fresh chives
2 T. chopped fresh parsley
1 T. capers, drained of their brine
1 to 2 T. chopped fresh thyme, stems removed

Whisk up a dressing of:
½ c. extra virgin olive oil
3 to 4 T. champagne vinegar
2 T. Dijon style mustard
2 T. honey
1 t. celery seed
Freshly ground pepper, to taste
Salt, to taste

Instructions:

Place small, same-sized, thin-skinned spuds in a medium sized pot in just two inches of salted water –one heaping tablespoon of salt should be enough. If needed, cut larger potatoes in half or quarters to match the size of the smallest potatoes in your batch. Cover the pot with a proper fitting lid and place over high heat, and then wait for the water to boil.

Ready a large bowl with ice cubes and cold water to create an icy bath, and set aside.

As soon as the potatoes have started boiling, reduce the heat to medium and replace the lid. Set a timer for fifteen minutes.

While the potatoes are cooking, whisk up the dressing ingredients and then prepare all other items as indicated in the recipe (chopped, diced, minced, etc.)

Even before the timer goes off, start checking the potatoes for your desired tenderness by poking a few of them with the point of a

sharp knife. If it pierces them fairly easily then they're ready. *Baby potatoes and Fingerling potatoes might be done even sooner than fifteen minutes so adjust the timing accordingly.* You're the one in control; don't overcook your potatoes.

Now firm but tender, quickly transfer them with a "spider" utensil or slotted spoon to the icy water. After three minutes, drain them thoroughly and let them dry on a cutting board. Then slice into bite-sized pieces.

Place the cut potatoes in a mixing bowl with the vegetables and capers and fold carefully with a wooden spoon or rubber spatula. Next, add the whisked dressing while continuing to gently fold everything together. Refrigerate until ready to enjoy.

Lemon Tarragon Potato Salad
Tart citrus pairs perfectly with fresh tarragon

Mayo free!

2½ lbs. potatoes
2 stalks fresh celery, diced
1 T. capers, drained of their brine

Whisk up a dressing of:
 ½ c. extra virgin olive oil
 3 T. white wine vinegar
 1 fresh lemon, fully zested plus all its juice
 2 T. chopped fresh tarragon, stems removed
 1 t. sugar
 Freshly ground pepper, to taste
 Salt, to taste

Instructions:

Place small, same-sized, thin-skinned spuds in a medium sized pot in just two inches of salted water –one heaping tablespoon of salt should be enough. If needed, cut larger potatoes in half or quarters to match the size of the smallest potatoes in your batch. Cover the pot with a proper fitting lid and place over high heat, and then wait for the water to boil.

Ready a large bowl with ice cubes and cold water to create an icy bath, and set aside.

As soon as the potatoes have started boiling, reduce the heat to medium and replace the lid. Set a timer for fifteen minutes.

While the potatoes are cooking, whisk up the dressing ingredients and then prepare all other items as indicated in the recipe (chopped, diced, minced, etc.)

Even before the timer goes off, start checking the potatoes for your desired tenderness by poking a few of them with the point of a sharp knife. If it pierces them fairly easily then they're ready. *Baby potatoes and Fingerling potatoes might be done even sooner than fifteen*

minutes so adjust the timing accordingly. You're the one in control; don't overcook your potatoes.

Now firm but tender, quickly transfer them with a "spider" utensil or slotted spoon to the icy water. After three minutes, drain them thoroughly and let them dry on a cutting board. Then slice into bite-sized pieces.

Place the cut potatoes in a mixing bowl with the celery and capers and fold carefully with a wooden spoon or rubber spatula. Next, add the whisked dressing while continuing to gently fold everything together. Refrigerate until ready to enjoy.

Creamy Lemon Tarragon Potato Salad
A creamy version of its cousin above...

2½ lbs. potatoes
2 stalks fresh celery, diced
1 T. capers, drained of their brine

Whisk up a dressing of:
½ c. mayonnaise
½ c. sour cream
1 T. olive oil
1 fresh lemon, fully zested plus *half* its juice
2 T. chopped fresh tarragon, stems removed
Freshly ground pepper, to taste
Salt, to taste

Instructions:

Place small, same-sized, thin-skinned spuds in a medium sized pot in just two inches of salted water –one heaping tablespoon of salt should be enough. If needed, cut larger potatoes in half or quarters to match the size of the smallest potatoes in your batch. Cover the pot with a proper fitting lid and place over high heat, and then wait for the water to boil.

Ready a large bowl with ice cubes and cold water to create an icy bath, and set aside.

As soon as the potatoes have started boiling, reduce the heat to medium and replace the lid. Set a timer for fifteen minutes.

While the potatoes are cooking, whisk up the dressing ingredients and then prepare all other items as indicated in the recipe (chopped, diced, minced, etc.)

Even before the timer goes off, start checking the potatoes for your desired tenderness by poking a few of them with the point of a sharp knife. If it pierces them fairly easily then they're ready. *Baby potatoes and Fingerling potatoes might be done even sooner than fifteen minutes so adjust the timing accordingly.* You're the one in control; don't overcook your potatoes.

Now firm but tender, quickly transfer them with a "spider" utensil or slotted spoon to the icy water. After three minutes, drain them thoroughly and let them dry on a cutting board. Then slice into bite-sized pieces.

Place the cut potatoes in a mixing bowl with the celery and capers and fold carefully with a wooden spoon or rubber spatula. Next, add the whisked dressing while continuing to gently fold everything together. Refrigerate until ready to enjoy.

Parisian Style Potato Salad
Serve this one warm as a unique side dish

Mayo free!

2½ lbs. potatoes
1 large fresh shallot, chopped
1 c. peas (fresh and blanched, or frozen and thawed)
8 mini Cornichon pickles, sliced

Whisk up a dressing of:
½ c. extra virgin olive oil
3 to 4 T. white wine vinegar
2 t. celery seed
1 T. grainy Dijon style mustard
1 T. chopped fresh dill
Freshly ground pepper, to taste
Salt, to taste

Instructions:

Place small, same-sized, thin-skinned spuds in a medium sized pot in just two inches of salted water –one heaping tablespoon of salt should be enough. If needed, cut larger potatoes in half or quarters to match the size of the smallest potatoes in your batch. Cover the pot with a proper fitting lid and place over high heat, and then wait for the water to boil.

Ready a large bowl with ice cubes and cold water to create an icy bath, and set aside.

As soon as the potatoes have started boiling, reduce the heat to medium and replace the lid. Set a timer for fifteen minutes.

While the potatoes are cooking, whisk up the dressing ingredients and then prepare all other items as indicated in the recipe (chopped, diced, minced, etc.)

Even before the timer goes off, start checking the potatoes for your desired tenderness by poking a few of them with the point of a sharp knife. If it pierces them fairly easily then they're ready. *Baby*

potatoes and Fingerling potatoes might be done even sooner than fifteen minutes so adjust the timing accordingly. You're the one in control; don't overcook your potatoes.

Now firm but tender, quickly transfer them with a "spider" utensil or slotted spoon to the icy water. After three minutes, drain them thoroughly and let them dry on a cutting board. Then slice into bite-sized pieces.

Place the cut potatoes in a mixing bowl with the other vegetables and fold carefully with a wooden spoon or rubber spatula. Next, add the whisked dressing while continuing to gently fold everything together. Refrigerate until ready to enjoy.

Potato salads
from around the world
are next!

International Styles

So many regions, so little time! Potato salads influenced by countries and places around the globe just might earn your admiration as much as they have mine. Here are few of my very favorite (and most creative) selections.

Quick note: These recipes may yield more dressing than you'll need –add it a bit at a time until you're satisfied with the "wetness" of your potato salad. Some people like it more on the drier side, but make yours how *you* want it.

Warm German Potato Salad
My favorite kind of potato salad

Mayo free!

2½ lbs. potatoes (If using Idaho Russets, peel and cut into thirds)
8 strips of bacon, cut in half to shorten (plus all the rendered fat)
Half of a Vidalia onion, diced
½ c. white wine vinegar
1½ T. grainy or Dijon style mustard
1½ T. sugar
1 T. chopped chives
½ t. celery seeds
-and melted bacon fat in the pan

Serve warm!

Instructions:

Begin by cooking the potatoes. Place small, same-sized spuds in a medium sized pot in just two inches of salted water –one heaping tablespoon of salt should be enough. If needed, cut larger potatoes in half or quarters to match the size of the smallest potatoes in your batch. Cover the pot with a proper fitting lid and place over high heat, and then wait for the water to boil.

As soon as the potatoes have started boiling, reduce the heat to medium and replace the lid. Set a timer for fifteen minutes.

Even before the timer goes off, start checking the potatoes for your desired tenderness by poking a few of them with the point of a sharp knife. If it pierces them fairly easily then they're ready.

Now firm but tender, quickly transfer them with a "spider" utensil or slotted spoon to a cutting board to let dry and cool down enough to touch. Then slice into bite-sized pieces if you haven't already.

In a large frying pan, cook the bacon over medium high heat until just crispy and set aside. To the fat in the pan add the diced onion and sauté until translucent. Then add the celery seed, sugar, mustard, and vinegar. Simmer until thickened slightly. Add the potatoes, chives, and crumpled bacon to the pan mixture and mix to coat. Serve warm.

Dutch Huzaren-Salade
Fresh apple adds an unexpected crunch and sweetness

2½ lbs. potatoes
2 hardboiled eggs, diced (prepared beforehand)
Half of a Vidalia onion, diced
4 medium pickled Gherkins, chopped
1 c. peas (fresh & blanched, or frozen & thawed)
1 c. diced ham
1 large apple, peeled, cored, and diced
1 T. chopped fresh parsley

Whisk up a dressing of:
¾ c. mayonnaise
3 T. apple cider vinegar
1 t. sugar
Freshly ground pepper, to taste
Salt, to taste

Instructions:

Place small, same-sized, thin-skinned spuds in a medium sized pot in just two inches of salted water –one heaping tablespoon of salt should be enough. If needed, cut larger potatoes in half or quarters to match the size of the smallest potatoes in your batch. Cover the pot with a proper fitting lid and place over high heat, and then wait for the water to boil.

Ready a large bowl with ice cubes and cold water to create an icy bath, and set aside.

As soon as the potatoes have started boiling, reduce the heat to medium and replace the lid. Set a timer for fifteen minutes.

While the potatoes are cooking, whisk up the dressing ingredients and then prepare all other items as indicated in the recipe (chopped, diced, minced, etc.)

Even before the timer goes off, start checking the potatoes for your desired tenderness by poking a few of them with the point of a sharp knife. If it pierces them fairly easily then they're ready. *Baby*

potatoes and Fingerling potatoes might be done even sooner than fifteen minutes so adjust the timing accordingly. You're the one in control; don't overcook your potatoes.

Now firm but tender, quickly transfer them with a "spider" utensil or slotted spoon to the icy water. After three minutes, drain them thoroughly and let them dry on a cutting board. Then slice into bite-sized pieces.

Place the cut potatoes in a mixing bowl with the other ingredients and fold carefully with a wooden spoon or rubber spatula. Next, add the whisked dressing while continuing to gently fold everything together. Refrigerate until ready to enjoy.

Spanish Chorizo Potato Salad
The mild spice and smokiness of Spanish flavors dominates this dish

Mayo free!

2½ lbs. potatoes
3 hardboiled eggs, diced (prepared beforehand)
2 stalks fresh celery, diced
1 c. cooked, diced Spanish chorizo sausage
2 T. chopped fresh parsley

Whisk up a dressing of:
  3/4 c. extra virgin olive oil
  3 to 4 T. sherry vinegar (for a true taste of Spain)
  1 T. sweet Spanish paprika
  Salt and freshly ground pepper, to taste

Instructions:

Place small, same-sized, thin-skinned spuds in a medium sized pot in just two inches of salted water –one heaping tablespoon of salt should be enough. If needed, cut larger potatoes in half or quarters to match the size of the smallest potatoes in your batch. Cover the pot with a proper fitting lid and place over high heat, and then wait for the water to boil.

Ready a large bowl with ice cubes and cold water to create an icy bath, and set aside.

As soon as the potatoes have started boiling, reduce the heat to medium and replace the lid. Set a timer for fifteen minutes.

While the potatoes are cooking, whisk up the dressing ingredients and then prepare all other items as indicated in the recipe (chopped, diced, minced, etc.)

Even before the timer goes off, start checking the potatoes for your desired tenderness by poking a few of them with the point of a sharp knife. If it pierces them fairly easily then they're ready. *Baby potatoes and Fingerling potatoes might be done even sooner than fifteen*

minutes so adjust the timing accordingly. You're the one in control; don't overcook your potatoes.

Now firm but tender, quickly transfer them with a "spider" utensil or slotted spoon to the icy water. After three minutes, drain them thoroughly and let them dry on a cutting board. Then slice into bite-sized pieces.

Place the cut potatoes in a mixing bowl with the other ingredients and fold carefully with a wooden spoon or rubber spatula. Next, add the whisked dressing while continuing to gently fold everything together. Refrigerate until ready to enjoy.

Warm Hungarian Potato Salad
A homemade paprika sauce lends authenticity of flavor

Mayo free!

2½ lbs. potatoes

Simmer on the stovetop until blended:
3 T. Smoked paprika
1 T. sugar
12 oz. tomato juice
Pinch of red pepper flakes, to taste (hot)
Freshly ground pepper, to taste
Salt only if needed
2 T. chopped fresh parsley

Topping: 6 T. cold sour cream, for a dollop on each serving

Serve warm

Instructions:

Place small, same-sized, thin-skinned spuds in a medium sized pot in just two inches of salted water –one heaping tablespoon of salt should be enough. If needed, cut larger potatoes in half or quarters to match the size of the smallest potatoes in your batch. Cover the pot with a proper fitting lid and place over high heat, and then wait for the water to boil.

As soon as the potatoes have started boiling, reduce the heat to medium and replace the lid. Set a timer for fifteen minutes.

While the potatoes are cooking, whisk up the dressing ingredients and then prepare all other items as indicated in the recipe (chopped, diced, minced, etc.)

Even before the timer goes off, start checking the potatoes for your desired tenderness by poking a few of them with the point of a sharp knife. If it pierces them fairly easily then they're ready. *Baby potatoes and Fingerling potatoes might be done even sooner than fifteen*

minutes so adjust the timing accordingly. You're the one in control; don't overcook your potatoes.

Now firm but tender, quickly transfer them with a "spider" utensil or slotted spoon to a cutting board to dry and cool down enough to touch. Then slice into bite-sized pieces.

Place the cut potatoes in a mixing bowl with the other vegetables and fold carefully with a wooden spoon or rubber spatula. Next, add the whisked dressing while continuing to gently fold everything together. Serve warm.

Asian Five-Spice Potato Salad
With the Far East flavors of ginger and five-spice

2½ lbs. potatoes
½ c. canned water chestnuts, chopped
3 stalks of fresh celery, diced
3 fresh scallions, chopped

  Whisk up a dressing of:
  1 c. mayonnaise
  1½ T. fresh pulverized ginger, (peel first and then use a food processor)
  2 T. "five-spice" seasoning
  Freshly ground pepper, to taste
  Salt, to taste

Instructions:

Place small, same-sized, thin-skinned spuds in a medium sized pot in just two inches of salted water –one heaping tablespoon of salt should be enough. If needed, cut larger potatoes in half or quarters to match the size of the smallest potatoes in your batch. Cover the pot with a proper fitting lid and place over high heat, and then wait for the water to boil.

Ready a large bowl with ice cubes and cold water to create an icy bath, and set aside.

As soon as the potatoes have started boiling, reduce the heat to medium and replace the lid. Set a timer for fifteen minutes.

While the potatoes are cooking, whisk up the dressing ingredients and then prepare all other items as indicated in the recipe (chopped, diced, minced, etc.)

Even before the timer goes off, start checking the potatoes for your desired tenderness by poking a few of them with the point of a sharp knife. If it pierces them fairly easily then they're ready. *Baby potatoes and Fingerling potatoes might be done even sooner than fifteen minutes so adjust the timing accordingly.* You're the one in control; don't overcook your potatoes.

Now firm but tender, quickly transfer them with a "spider" utensil or slotted spoon to the icy water. After three minutes, drain them thoroughly and let them dry on a cutting board. Then slice into bite-sized pieces.

Place the cut potatoes in a mixing bowl with the other vegetables and fold carefully with a wooden spoon or rubber spatula. Next, add the whisked dressing while continuing to gently fold everything together. Refrigerate until ready to enjoy.

Russian Potato Salad
The sharpness of horseradish makes this one a standout

2½ lbs. potatoes
3 stalks of fresh celery, diced
¾ c. peas (fresh and blanched or frozen and thawed)
2 T. chopped fresh chives

Whisk up a dressing of:
½ c. sour cream
½ c. mayonnaise
2 to 3 T. prepared horseradish (spicy!)
Salt, to taste

Instructions:

Place small, same-sized, thin-skinned spuds in a medium sized pot in just two inches of salted water –one heaping tablespoon of salt should be enough. If needed, cut larger potatoes in half or quarters to match the size of the smallest potatoes in your batch. Cover the pot with a proper fitting lid and place over high heat, and then wait for the water to boil.

Ready a large bowl with ice cubes and cold water to create an icy bath, and set aside.

As soon as the potatoes have started boiling, reduce the heat to medium and replace the lid. Set a timer for fifteen minutes.

While the potatoes are cooking, whisk up the dressing ingredients and then prepare all other items as indicated in the recipe (chopped, diced, minced, etc.)

Even before the timer goes off, start checking the potatoes for your desired tenderness by poking a few of them with the point of a sharp knife. If it pierces them fairly easily then they're ready. *Baby potatoes and Fingerling potatoes might be done even sooner than fifteen minutes so adjust the timing accordingly.* You're the one in control; don't overcook your potatoes.

Now firm but tender, quickly transfer them with a "spider" utensil or slotted spoon to the icy water. After three minutes, drain

them thoroughly and let them dry on a cutting board. Then slice into bite-sized pieces.

Place the cut potatoes in a mixing bowl with the other vegetables and fold carefully with a wooden spoon or rubber spatula. Next, add the whisked dressing while continuing to gently fold everything together. Refrigerate until ready to enjoy.

Indian Curried Potato Salad
Exotic, with a sweet and spicy flavor profile

Mayo free!

2½ lbs. potatoes
3 stalks of fresh celery, diced
½ c. golden raisins
3 T. toasted, sliced almonds
½ c. dried apricots, roughly chopped

Whisk up a dressing of:
1 c. plain Greek style yogurt
1 to 2 T. curry powder
1 to 2 T. honey
Salt, to taste

Instructions:

Place small, same-sized, thin-skinned spuds in a medium sized pot in just two inches of salted water –one heaping tablespoon of salt should be enough. If needed, cut larger potatoes in half or quarters to match the size of the smallest potatoes in your batch. Cover the pot with a proper fitting lid and place over high heat, and then wait for the water to boil.

Ready a large bowl with ice cubes and cold water to create an icy bath, and set aside.

As soon as the potatoes have started boiling, reduce the heat to medium and replace the lid. Set a timer for fifteen minutes.

While the potatoes are cooking, whisk up the dressing ingredients and then prepare all other items as indicated in the recipe (chopped, diced, minced, etc.)

Even before the timer goes off, start checking the potatoes for your desired tenderness by poking a few of them with the point of a sharp knife. If it pierces them fairly easily then they're ready. *Baby potatoes and Fingerling potatoes might be done even sooner than fifteen*

minutes so adjust the timing accordingly. You're the one in control; don't overcook your potatoes.

Now firm but tender, quickly transfer them with a "spider" utensil or slotted spoon to the icy water. After three minutes, drain them thoroughly and let them dry on a cutting board. Then slice into bite-sized pieces.

Place the cut potatoes in a mixing bowl with the other ingredients and fold carefully with a wooden spoon or rubber spatula. Next, add the whisked dressing while continuing to gently fold everything together. Refrigerate until ready to enjoy.

Mexican Style Potato Salad
A bright lime crema is the star of this potato salad

Mayo free!

2½ lbs. potatoes
1 fresh red bell pepper, diced, with pith removed
1 c. loose cooked corn, drained
Half of a red onion, diced
2 T. chopped fresh cilantro, larger stems removed

  Whisk up a dressing of:
  ¾ c. sour cream
  1 to 2 fresh jalapeño peppers, seeds and pith removed, diced
  2 fresh limes, fully zested plus all their juice
  Freshly ground pepper, to taste

Topping: 1 c. Mexican Cotija or Queso Fresca cheese, crumbled

Cotija cheese is a bit salty, so don't add additional salt until after tasting the finished potato salad! Salting the boiling water for the raw potatoes is fine.

Instructions:

Place small, same-sized, thin-skinned spuds in a medium sized pot in just two inches of salted water –one heaping tablespoon of salt should be enough. If needed, cut larger potatoes in half or quarters to match the size of the smallest potatoes in your batch. Cover the pot with a proper fitting lid and place over high heat, and then wait for the water to boil.

Ready a large bowl with ice cubes and cold water to create an icy bath, and set aside.

As soon as the potatoes have started boiling, reduce the heat to medium and replace the lid. Set a timer for fifteen minutes.

While the potatoes are cooking, whisk up the dressing ingredients and then prepare all other items as indicated in the recipe (chopped, diced, minced, etc.)

Even before the timer goes off, start checking the potatoes for your desired tenderness by poking a few of them with the point of a sharp knife. If it pierces them fairly easily then they're ready. *Baby potatoes and Fingerling potatoes might be done even sooner than fifteen minutes so adjust the timing accordingly.* You're the one in control; don't overcook your potatoes.

Now firm but tender, quickly transfer them with a "spider" utensil or slotted spoon to the icy water. After three minutes, drain them thoroughly and let them dry on a cutting board. Then slice into bite-sized pieces.

Place the cut potatoes in a mixing bowl with the other vegetables and fold carefully with a wooden spoon or rubber spatula. Next, add the whisked dressing while continuing to gently fold everything together. Refrigerate until ready to enjoy and then top with the crumbled cheese.

Smoky Chipotle Potato Salad
A smoked jalapeno dressing makes this one irresistible

2½ lbs. potatoes
1 fresh green bell pepper, diced, with pith removed
1 c. loose cooked corn, drained
½ c. canned black beans, rinsed and drained
2 T. chopped fresh cilantro, larger stems removed

Whisk up a spicy dressing of:
½ c. mayonnaise
½ c. sour cream
1 fresh lime, fully zested plus all its juice
2 T. chopped, prepared chipotle peppers in sauce (canned)
Salt, to taste

Topping: 6 T. sour cream, for a dollop on each serving

Instructions:

Place small, same-sized, thin-skinned spuds in a medium sized pot in just two inches of salted water –one heaping tablespoon of salt should be enough. If needed, cut larger potatoes in half or quarters to match the size of the smallest potatoes in your batch. Cover the pot with a proper fitting lid and place over high heat, and then wait for the water to boil.

Ready a large bowl with ice cubes and cold water to create an icy bath, and set aside.

As soon as the potatoes have started boiling, reduce the heat to medium and replace the lid. Set a timer for fifteen minutes.

While the potatoes are cooking, whisk up the dressing ingredients and then prepare all other items as indicated in the recipe (chopped, diced, minced, etc.)

Even before the timer goes off, start checking the potatoes for your desired tenderness by poking a few of them with the point of a sharp knife. If it pierces them fairly easily then they're ready. *Baby potatoes and Fingerling potatoes might be done even sooner than fifteen*

minutes so adjust the timing accordingly. You're the one in control; don't overcook your potatoes.

Now firm but tender, quickly transfer them with a "spider" utensil or slotted spoon to the icy water. After three minutes, drain them thoroughly and let them dry on a cutting board. Then slice into bite-sized pieces.

Place the cut potatoes in a mixing bowl with the other vegetables and fold carefully with a wooden spoon or rubber spatula. Next, add the whisked dressing while continuing to gently fold everything together. Refrigerate until ready to enjoy and then top each serving with a dollop of sour cream.

Hawaiian Sweet & Sour Potato Salad
Pineapple vinaigrette wakes this one right up

Mayo free!

2½ lbs. potatoes
2 fresh scallions, chopped
½ c. roasted red peppers, diced
1 c. crispy, chopped bacon (prepared beforehand)
½ c. chopped pineapple

Whisk up a dressing of:
½ c. extra virgin olive oil
2 T. red wine vinegar
¼ c. pineapple juice
1 T. prepared yellow mustard
1 t. sugar
Salt and freshly ground pepper, to taste

Topping: ½ c. roasted, chopped Macadamia nuts, divided up to top each serving

Instructions:

Place small, same-sized, thin-skinned spuds in a medium sized pot in just two inches of salted water –one heaping tablespoon of salt should be enough. If needed, cut larger potatoes in half or quarters to match the size of the smallest potatoes in your batch. Cover the pot with a proper fitting lid and place over high heat, and then wait for the water to boil.

Ready a large bowl with ice cubes and cold water to create an icy bath, and set aside.

As soon as the potatoes have started boiling, reduce the heat to medium and replace the lid. Set a timer for fifteen minutes.

While the potatoes are cooking, whisk up the dressing ingredients and then prepare all other items as indicated in the recipe (chopped, diced, minced, etc.)

Even before the timer goes off, start checking the potatoes for your desired tenderness by poking a few of them with the point of a sharp knife. If it pierces them fairly easily then they're ready. *Baby potatoes and Fingerling potatoes might be done even sooner than fifteen minutes so adjust the timing accordingly.* You're the one in control; don't overcook your potatoes.

Now firm but tender, quickly transfer them with a "spider" utensil or slotted spoon to the icy water. After three minutes, drain them thoroughly and let them dry on a cutting board. Then slice into bite-sized pieces.

Place the cut potatoes in a mixing bowl with the other vegetables, pineapple, and bacon and fold carefully with a wooden spoon or rubber spatula. Next, add the whisked dressing while continuing to gently fold everything together. Refrigerate until ready to enjoy and then top each serving with the chopped nuts.

Vietnamese Sriracha Potato Salad
The spiciness of chilies and garlic add terrific flavor

2½ lbs. potatoes
3 T. chopped fresh cilantro, larger stems removed
2 stalks fresh celery, chopped

Whisk up a dressing of:
¾ c. mayonnaise
1 T. extra virgin olive oil
3 to 4 T. Sriracha sauce (hot)
Add salt to taste, if needed

Instructions:

Place small, same-sized, thin-skinned spuds in a medium sized pot in just two inches of salted water –one heaping tablespoon of salt should be enough. If needed, cut larger potatoes in half or quarters to match the size of the smallest potatoes in your batch. Cover the pot with a proper fitting lid and place over high heat, and then wait for the water to boil.

Ready a large bowl with ice cubes and cold water to create an icy bath, and set aside.

As soon as the potatoes have started boiling, reduce the heat to medium and replace the lid. Set a timer for fifteen minutes.

While the potatoes are cooking, whisk up the dressing ingredients and then prepare all other items as indicated in the recipe (chopped, diced, minced, etc.)

Even before the timer goes off, start checking the potatoes for your desired tenderness by poking a few of them with the point of a sharp knife. If it pierces them fairly easily then they're ready. *Baby potatoes and Fingerling potatoes might be done even sooner than fifteen minutes so adjust the timing accordingly.* You're the one in control; don't overcook your potatoes.

Now firm but tender, quickly transfer them with a "spider" utensil or slotted spoon to the icy water. After three minutes, drain

them thoroughly and let them dry on a cutting board. Then slice into bite-sized pieces.

Place the cut potatoes in a mixing bowl with the other vegetables and fold carefully with a wooden spoon or rubber spatula. Next, add the whisked dressing while continuing to gently fold everything together. Refrigerate until ready to enjoy or serve warm.

Calling all Cooks

Thank you so much for your interest in my recipes. It was great fun bringing you these wonderful flavor combinations. If you enjoyed *Life-Changing Potato Salads in 30 Minutes Flat*, please take a moment to leave a short customer review on Amazon so that your rating will count for me. Even a few sentences would be helpful, and much appreciated.

~Grace

Books by Grace Légere

Life-Changing Salad Dressings in 3 Minutes Flat

Life-Changing Compound Butters in 3 Minutes Flat

Life-Changing Potato Salads in 30 Minutes Flat

Life-Changing Salsa Fresca in 30 Minutes or Less

Life-Changing Avocado Toast in No Time Flat

Made in the USA
Monee, IL
20 May 2022

96706703R00074